CURLING

GLOBAL CITIZENS: OLYMPIC SPORTS

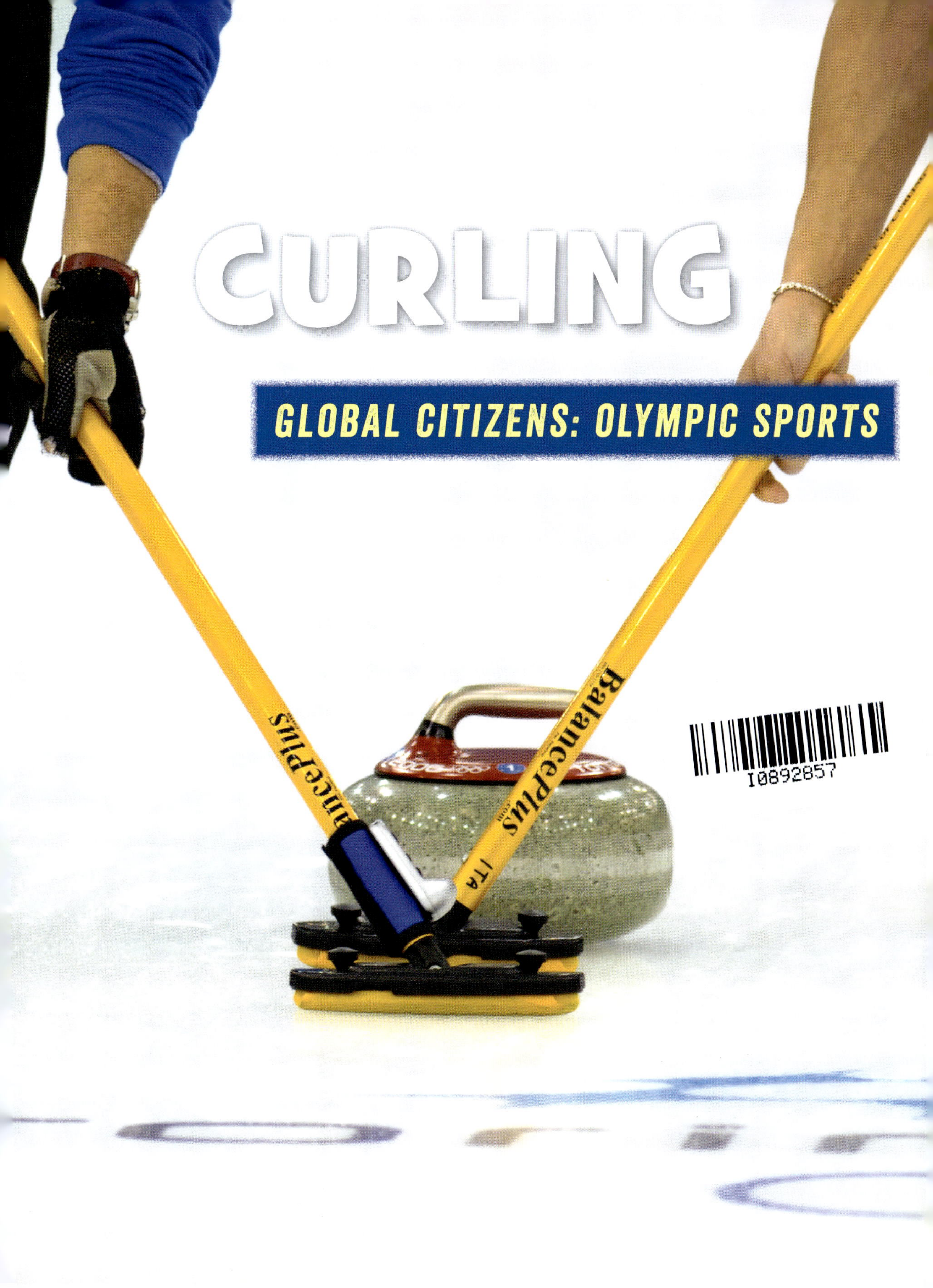

CHERRY LAKE Publishing

Published in the United States of America by Cherry Lake Publishing
Ann Arbor, Michigan
www.cherrylakepublishing.com

Content Adviser: Liv Williams, Editor, www.iLivExtreme.com
Reading Adviser: Marla Conn MS, Ed., Literacy specialist, Read-Ability, Inc.

Photo Credits: ©Paolo Bona / Shutterstock.com, cover, 15; ©Michael715 / Shutterstock.com, 5; ©Painting by Roger Griffith [1860] / Wikimedia Commons / Public Domain, 6; ©Alfaguarilla / Shutterstock.com, 7, 8, 21; ©bodrumsurf / Shutterstock.com, 10; ©Jamie Roach / Shutterstock.com, 13; ©Chase N. / flickr.com, 14, 16, 23, 27; ©KoreaKHW / Shutterstock.com, 19; ©Brian Holsclaw / flickr.com, 20; ©Phil Stafford / Shutterstock.com, 22; ©Olha Insight / Shutterstock.com, 24; ©ID1974 / Shutterstock.com, 28

Library of Congress Cataloging-in-Publication Data

Names: Labrecque, Ellen, author.
Title: Curling / by Ellen Labrecque.
Description: Ann Arbor, Michigan : Cherry Lake Publishing, 2018. | Series: Global citizens: Olympic sports | Includes bibliographical references and index.
Identifiers: LCCN 2017033454 | ISBN 9781534107540 (hardcover) | ISBN 9781534109520 (pdf) | ISBN 9781534108530 (pbk.) | ISBN 9781534120518 (hosted ebook)
Subjects: LCSH: Curling—Juvenile literature. | Winter Olympics—Juvenile literature.
Classification: LCC GV845 .L33 2018 | DDC 796.964—dc23
LC record available at https://lccn.loc.gov/2017033454

Cherry Lake Publishing would like to acknowledge the work of The Partnership for 21st Century Learning. Please visit *www.p21.org* for more information.

Printed in the United States of America
Corporate Graphics

ABOUT THE AUTHOR

Ellen Labrecque has written over 100 books for children. She loves the Olympics and has attended both the Winter and Summer Games as a reporter for magazines and television. She lives in Yardley, Pennsylvania, with her husband, Jeff, and her two young "editors," Sam and Juliet. When she isn't writing, she is running, hiking, and reading.

TABLE OF CONTENTS

CHAPTER 1

History: Curling

The first Winter Olympics was held in Chamonix, France, from January 25 to February 5, 1924. It included 258 athletes from 16 different countries competing in 16 events. Since then, the Winter Olympics has been held every 4 years in a number of countries. (The Games were skipped in 1940 and 1944 during World War II.) As the Games progressed, more competitors and events were added. Fast-forward to the 2014 Winter Games held in Sochi, Russia. There were 2,873 competitors from 88 different countries competing in 98 events. That's a lot more competitors and events!

Curling is played with a broom and special granite stones.

From jaw-dropping aerial flips in skiing to lightning-speed action in hockey, the Winter Games display some of the most unbelievable sports and athletes. Curling is a sport sometimes referred to as "chess on ice" because it relies on complex strategy. It is one of the oldest sports in the Winter Olympics.

Women curling in Scotland in 1860.

The Story of Curling

Curling is a lot like shuffleboard. But instead of pushing the weighted disk, or stone, on a dry surface, athletes push it on ice using brooms! The sport started in the 16th century in Scotland. People played on frozen ponds and lakes. The first curling club, the Grand Caledonian Curling Club, was formed in 1838. This was also the year the official rules of the game were made. Teams consist of two or four players, or curlers. Curlers slide giant stones (42 pounds, or 19 kilograms) across the ice at a

Curlers wear shoes with two different soles!

A curler's back foot pushes against the hack before releasing the stone.

target 126 feet (38.4 meters) away. After the stone is released, two curlers sweep the ice in front of the stone to control its speed and direction. The sport is named "curling" because of the way the disk "curls," or curves, when the players sweep the ice in front of it.

Curling was included in the first Winter Olympics. But then it was excluded from the Games for 16 straight seasons. It was later reintroduced at the 1998 Games in Nagano, Japan, and has been part of the Winter Games ever since.

Curlers and Their Roles

Lead *Throws the first two stones and sweeps the following six*

Second *Sweeps the first two stones and the final four; throws the next two stones after the Lead*

Third *Throws the next two stones after the Second; sets up the final two stones for the Skip*

Skip *Captain of the team who determines the strategy; throws the final two stones*

Note: *In the Mixed Doubles event, the team consists of two players (one male and one female) who alternate throwing and sweeping the stones. The two-player team delivers six stones instead of eight.*

Curlers sweep the ice in front of the stone in order for it to "curl."

Curling at Any Age

Most Olympic athletes are at their peak performance when they are in their mid- to late 20s, and they retire by their late 30s to early 40s. Curling, though, is a sport you can play at almost any age. In fact, the oldest Winter Olympic medalist was curler Carl August Kronlund. At age 58, he won the silver medal for Sweden at the 1924 Games. The oldest gold medal winner is Robin Welsh. At age 54, he helped beat Sweden to win the gold for Great Britain in 1924.

Developing Claims and Using Evidence

The ice surface in curling is not smooth. Water is sprayed on the ice to give it a "pebbled surface." The sweepers on each team sweep the ice with brooms to make the stone go faster and curve one way or another. But high-tech brooms were recently invented that made it even easier to direct the stone and make it go at the exact right speed. Some curlers did not like the new brooms at all. They thought it was cheating. Go on the Internet and read all about these new brooms. Do you think they should be allowed? Why or why not?

CHAPTER 2

Geography: Canada Rules Curling!

Many countries all over the world curl. Many also do not. At the 2014 Winter Olympics, only 100 athletes from 12 different countries participated in curling. Compare this to the 327 athletes from 74 nations who participated in one of the alpine skiing events. That's a big difference!

Around the world, 1.5 million people participate in curling in 35 countries. But 80 percent of these curlers are in Canada! More than 1,000 curling clubs can be found across that nation. Not surprisingly, Canada has been one of the top competitors

Kaitlyn Lawes of Canada was on the first Olympic women's team to go the whole Games undefeated when they won gold in 2014.

The Canadian team discuss strategy at the 2010 Games in Vancouver.

for the past five Winter Olympic seasons in both the men's and women's events. Canada has won two medals at each Winter Games since the sport was reintroduced at the 1998 Olympics. The country has a total of five gold, three silver, and two bronze medals. To date, Switzerland is the only other country to win at least one curling medal in each Olympics since 1998 (one gold, two silver, two bronze).

Stones must touch the outer ring or anything within that area in order to score a point.

Debbie McCormick of Madison, Wisconsin, participated in three Olympic Games.

Improving the US Team

Despite having the second-highest number of curlers in the world, with 15,000 athletes playing in one of 135 clubs across the nation, the United States has won only one Olympic medal in curling. That was when the men's team placed third at the 2006 Games in Turin, Italy. One reason for this may be because the best curlers aren't picked to go to the Olympics. The United States selects the best teams, not the best individuals. Even if there were better curlers on other teams, the United States wouldn't break up a team to form a new one. The United States Curling Association is working on changing this rule for future Olympics, but it hasn't happened yet.

Gathering and Evaluating Sources

Wisconsin has the most active curling clubs in the United States, with 31 indoor and outdoor playing areas. Arizona has one club, but doesn't have any place to play or practice. Using the Internet and your local library, make a list of the top states with the highest number of curling clubs. Make a list of states that have very few or none at all. Why do you think some states have significantly more clubs? Use the information you find to support your answer.

CHAPTER 3

Civics: Olympic Pride

Hosting the Olympic Games can be a big source of pride for the city and the people who live there. It gives the citizens a chance to show off where they live to the entire world. The athletes and fans who come to the Games spend a lot of money there, too. One of the biggest ways the host country shows off is at the opening and closing ceremonies. At the 2018 Winter Olympics, curling starts the day before the opening ceremonies and doesn't finish until the last day of the Games. It is the only sport that has an event every day of the Games!

The 2018 Olympic curling events will be held at the Gangneung Ice Arena in PyeongChang, South Korea.

Bagpipe players opened the Olympic curling events at the 2010 Games.

People Love Curling

At the 2014 Winter Olympics, curling was the sport most **tweeted** about at the Games for 12 of the 16 days of competition. It also did well on television. On the first day that NBC began covering curling at the Games, it had 5 million viewers in the United States alone! The men's final was the second-highest-rated program in Canada *and* the United States during the Games!

The Japanese men's team will compete in the 2018 Games for the first time since the 1998 Nagano Olympics.

Davis also plans to attend the 2018 Games to cheer on the US curling team.

Sweden beat Canada for gold at the 2010 Games.

Curling's Biggest Fan

Tight end Vernon Davis of the Washington Redskins is one of the biggest stars in the National Football League (NFL). He is also one of the biggest curling fans around. He attended the 2010 Games in Vancouver, Canada, and fell in love with the sport. He also plays on his own in his free time. Davis now serves as the unofficial team captain for the US Curling Team. He traveled all the way to Sochi, Russia, for the 2014 Games to cheer on the team as well as to promote the sport. "There is no NFL player that promotes curling but me," says Davis. "And that's pretty cool."

At the 2014 Games, the "Buff Boys" of Canada brought home gold.

The "Buff Boys"

When curling first started, curlers weren't known to be the fittest athletes. In fact, some were overweight and out of shape. But the Canadian men's team at the 2014 Games changed all that. They became known as the "Buff Boys" for their muscular arms and legs. They won gold. Canadian fans went crazy for them. Curling announcer Mike Harris called them the "fittest athletes at the Games."

Developing Claims

Now that you know more about curling, do you think it is important to be in top physical shape? Does the sport seem to require it? Why or why not?

CHAPTER 4

Economics: The Cost of Curling

Hosting the Olympic Games costs a lot of money. Sochi, Russia, the host of the 2014 Winter Olympics, spent $14 million on the curling **venue** alone! This cost didn't include any of the other venues or even the stadium for the opening and closing ceremonies. How do Olympic host cities earn back most of this money?

The Fans

Olympic **tourists** spend money by staying in hotels, buying souvenirs, and eating in the city's restaurants. As curling has become more popular, more people are willing to buy tickets to watch the sport in person. Tickets for the 2018 Games in South Korea during key matches cost close to $200!

A long line of fans forms outside the 2010 Olympic curling arena.

The Ambassadors

Olympic cities ask athletes to be **ambassadors** for their Games. The athletes promote the Olympics to fans around the world. One of the ambassadors of the 2018 Games is **Paralympic** curling athlete Kim Hak-sung of South Korea. He won a silver medal at the 2010 Paralympics in Vancouver, Canada. This was the first time South Korea won a medal in this sport. Kim is one of his country's most famous athletes and was also one of the torchbearers at the 2014 Paralympics.

The Slovakia Paralympic team prepares to release the stone.

Taking Informed Action

Do you want to learn more about the Winter Olympics and curling? There are many different organizations that you can explore. Check them out online. Here are three to help you start your search:

- *Team USA—USA Curling: Learn more about the US Curling Team on its official Website.*
- *Olympic—Curling: Find out more about the history of curling at the Olympics.*
- *NBC Olympics: Stay updated on all things related to the Winter Olympics.*

The Sponsors

Advertisers like Coca-Cola and McDonald's pay a lot of money to sponsor the Olympics. Their signs and logos appear on television in commercials and on boards all over the venues. Clothing companies supply the uniforms and the outfits for the opening and closing ceremonies. Curlers are known to dress with style—especially the men's curling team from Norway. They wear crazy-colorful pants when they compete. It is no surprise that the company that makes these eccentric pants is called Loudmouth! You can buy these pants, but one pair will run you over $100!

Communicating Conclusions

Before reading this book, did you know a lot about curling and the Winter Olympics? Now that you know more, do you think curling is more interesting and exciting than you originally thought? How would you get people in the United States to watch and participate in curling more? Share what you learned with friends at school or with your family at home.

Think About It

When people think of dangerous Olympic sports, curling may not often come to mind. But at the 2010 Winter Olympics, 4 percent of curlers were injured. According to this statistic, this means curling is riskier than six other Olympic sports, including ski jumping, speed skating, and luge! What do you think makes curling more dangerous than these other sports? What areas of the body are curlers more likely to injure? Use the data you find from the Internet and your local library to support your answers.

For More Information

Further Reading

Wallechinsky, David, and Jaime Loucky. *The Complete Book of the Winter Olympics.* Hertford, NC: Crossroad Press, 2014.

Waxman, Laura Hamilton. *Ice Hockey and Curling.* Mankato, MN: Amicus Ink, 2017.

Wyman, Ted. *Ice Gold: Canada's Curling Champions.* Toronto: ECW Press, 2014.

Websites

The International Olympic Committee
https://www.olympic.org/the-ioc
Discover how the IOC works to build a better world through sports.

Team USA—Curling
http://www.teamusa.org/USA-Curling
Learn all about the US Olympics team.

World Curling Federation
www.worldcurling.org
Find out more about curling competitions all over the world.

GLOSSARY

ambassadors (am-BAS-uh-derz) representatives for something, like the Olympics

Paralympic (par-uh-LIM-pik) an international competition, like the Olympics, but for physically disabled athletes

tourists (TOOR-ists) people who are traveling for pleasure

tweeted (TWEET-id) posted a message on Twitter, an online message service

venue (VEN-yoo) the place of an action or event

INDEX